AF237729

Hypnosis for Beginners

Experiments, Connections and Applications in Magic

Contact: www.HarryEilenstein.de
Harry.Eilenstein@web.de
Harry Eilenstein at youtube

Imprint: Copyright: 2011 by Harry Eilenstein – All rights reserved, including but not limited to that of translation. No part of this book may be reproduced, translated, stored in a retrieval system, or transmitted in any form or by any means, electronic, mechanical, photocopying, recording, or otherwise, without the prior written permission of the author and the publisher.

Production and publishing house: BoD - Books on Demand, Norderstedt

ISBN: 9783753454634

Table of Contents

I What is Hypnosis?   6
    1. The "classical hypnosis   6
    2. Sleep talkers and sleepwalkers   6
    3. Dominant people   6
    4. Mass hypnosis   7
    5. A model of consciousness   8

II Methods of Hypnotizing   9
    1. The attitude of the hypnotist   9
    2. Hypnosis by words   9
    3. The "path" of hypnosis   14
    4. Hypnosis by gestures   16
    5. Hypnosis by life force   17
    6. Hypnosis by telepathy   19

III Possible Applications   21
    1. Research of the psyche   21
    2. Healing of the psyche   22
    3. Healing of the body   22
    4. Solving of crimes etc.   22
    5. Research of former incarnations   23
    6. Research of magical possibilities   24
    7. Commanding actions   26

IV The Depth of the Hypnotic State   28

V Waking up from Hypnosis   30
    1. Awakening by words   30
    2. Awakening by life force   31
    3. Independent awakening   32
33
VI The Side Effects of Hypnotizing   33
    1. One-time hypnosis   33
    2. Frequent hypnosis   33
    3. Alternatives to hypnosis   34

VII   Experiences with Hypnosis   **36**

VIII   Hypnosis-like Processes   **39**
    1. Transfer of consciousness   39
    2. Darshan   40
    3. Phowa   42
    4. Possession   43
    5. Hypnosis fight   43
    6. Expansion of consciousness   44
    7. Spiritus familiaris   45
    8. Levitation experiment   47
    9. The "Hepp" experiment   48
  10. A Shaolin experiment   49
  11. Advertising and propaganda   49

IX   A Hypnosis Model   **50**

    Book List   52

I What is Hypnosis?

I 1. "Classical Hypnosis"

Hypnosis is a state of the psyche and consciousness that does not usually occur in everyday life.

In "classical hypnosis", the hypnotist takes over the function of the waking consciousness of the hypnotized person, who thus enters a sleep-like state. In this state, the hypnotist can talk to the hypnotized person – however, he does not have the waking consciousness of the hypnotized person as "interlocutor", but only the subconsciousness of the hypnotized person. The hypnotized person is in a kind of dream state – more precisely in a "waking dream", since he is without waking consciousness but responsive.

I 2. Sleep talkers and sleep walkers

The only occasion on which a person naturally enters a state of hypnosis is when speaking in sleep. When questions are asked of a person speaking in sleep, that person answers those questions truthfully, because he answers not from his waking consciousness, but from his subconsciousness.

The extended version of these "sleep-talks" is sleep-walking, in which moving in sleep is added to talking in sleep. Some sleepwalkers can be asked to do something specific, which they then follow.

These two "natural hypnotic states" occur because the cerebellum does not sufficiently separate the inner dream images from the motor centers in the brain. This separation usually causes that when one dreams of running, one does not actually get up and start running.

I 3. Dominant people

There are people who immediately completely fill every room they enter. These people are usually rather dominant and often have a Scorpio Ascendant or Pluto in the first house of their chart. When such a person enters the room, one forgets what one actually wanted and leaves oneself largely to the other person's guidance of the situation.

This phenomenon is closely related to hypnosis – only that the people "hypnotized" in this way remain awake. However, the people in this "awake hypnosis" have largely given up the control of their actions.

Often these dominant people also have a manipulative way of speaking, i.e. they do not aim with their speaking to realize something together with the other person, but want to reach a certain goal with their words, i.e. to move others to a certain behavior. Most politicians belong to this sort of dominant people – "alpha males" and "alpha females".

I 4.   Mass hypnosis

In a mass hypnosis, such a dominant person takes a central position and directs a large crowd of people listening to him entirely toward himself – they are fixated on the speaker, he puts them under his spell, he extends his consciousness to them.

Such mass hypnosis can be found especially at large political events in dictatorships – they serve to subjugate people. Often these large-scale events are supported by the architecture of the place where the speech is held, by the lighting, by marches and stagings. The most important element is, of course, the will, the oratory, the facial expressions and the gestures of the speaker.

This "Gleichschaltung", as this technique was called in the "Third Reich", is the suppression and replacement of the alert and independently deciding ego of the listeners by the dominant ego of the dictator.

Successful talk show hosts, revolutionary leaders, generals etc. also need the ability to dominantly direct the mood of a group.

Hypnosis-like states obviously occur much more often in everyday life than one normally assumes …

I 5. A model of consciousness

There are four forms of consciousness in normal life:

- the deep sleep consciousness, which is like a white screen on which images can appear, or like silence in which a sound can be heard;

- the dream consciousness (subconsciousness), which contains all the perceptions and memories of the psyche concerned;

- the waking consciousness, which directs one's behavior in everyday life;

- and the ecstatic state, which manifests itself primarily in fear and pleasure.

These four forms of consciousness work together and have an effective division of labor:

- Deep sleep is the unlit house that provides the space.

- The subconscious mind is the archive in this house, which contains all the information and is only rather dimly lit.

- The waking consciousness is a desk in an office in this house, where there is a ceiling lamp that makes all the things in this room visible – that is where all the currently important informations are, that is, all the contents of consciousness that are needed in the present situation.

- The ecstasy state is the bright desk lamp that is turned on from time to time and that brightly illuminates a single object an the desk in the office, a single content of consciousness.

In addition to these four consciousnesses, there is the collective sub-consciousness, which in this picture can be seen as the city in which the house is located. The houses in this city are telepathically connected to each other by telephone lines – strictly speaking, the archives, i.e. the subconsciousnesses of the people are telepathically connected to each other.

II   Methods of Hypnotizing

Hypnosis is effected by will, by words, by gestures, by directing the life force and by telepathy.

II 1.   The Hypnotist's Attitude

Hypnosis requires of the hypnotist not only that he speaks a few mysterious words, have a piercing look, and make some mysterious gestures …

The most important thing is the hypnotist's determination to hypnotize his counter-part, i.e. to "take direction over the other person". Thus, the hypnotist consciously enters into an attitude of dominance over the person he wants to hypnotize. This is not only a slight superiority, but a (temporary) absolute domination over the other person – just complete dominance. A hypnotist should therefore have a strong will.

Without this dominant attitude nothing works at all in hypnosis …

II 2.   Hypnosis by words

The "classical hypnosis formula" is quite simple: One goes through the individual body parts from bottom to top and says one after the other that they are relaxed, heavy, warm and tired.

The following text is the detailed version, which can be used if you want to use almost only words for hypnosis. This text can also be changed and shortened according to the needs. As with almost all things, a little experimentation is extremely beneficial – so you can find out your own style, in this case the way in which you find hypnotizing easiest.

"Your right foot is completely relaxed,
Your right calf is completely relaxed,
Your right knee is completely relaxed,
Your right thigh is completely relaxed;

Your left foot is completely relaxed,
Your left calf is completely relaxed,
Your left knee is completely relaxed,
Your left thigh is completely relaxed;

Your buttocks are completely relaxed,
Your abdomen is completely relaxed,
Your belly is completely relaxed,
Your chest is completely relaxed,
Your lower back is completely relaxed,
Your upper back is completely relaxed,
Your shoulders are completely relaxed;

Your right hand is completely relaxed,
Your right forearm is completely relaxed,
Your right elbow is completely relaxed,
Your right upper arm is completely relaxed;

Your left hand is completely relaxed,
Your left forearm is completely relaxed,
Your left elbow is completely relaxed,
Your left upper arm is completely relaxed;

Your neck is completely relaxed,
your throat is completely relaxed,
Your neck is completely relaxed,
The back of your head is completely relaxed,
The top of your head is completely relaxed,
Your ears are completely relaxed,
Your lower jaw is completely relaxed,
Your upper jaw is completely relaxed,
Your cheeks are completely relaxed,
Your nose is completely relaxed,
Your forehead is completely relaxed,
Your eyes are completely relaxed.

Your right foot is very warm,
Your right calf is very warm,
Your right knee is all warm,
Your right thigh is all warm;

Your left foot is all warm,
Your left calf is all warm,
Your left knee is all warm,
Your left thigh is all warm;

Your buttocks are all warm,
Your abdomen is all warm,
Your belly is all warm,
Your chest is all warm,
Your lower back is all warm,
Your upper back is all warm,
Your shoulders are all warm;

Your right hand is all warm,
Your right forearm is all warm,
Your right elbow is all warm,
Your right upper arm is all warm;

Your left hand is all warm,
Your left forearm is all warm,
Your left elbow is all warm,
Your left upper arm is all warm;

Your neck is all warm,
Your throat is all warm,
Your neck is all warm,
The back of your head is all warm,
The top of your head is all warm,
Your ears are all warm,
Your lower jaw is all warm,
Your upper jaw is all warm,
Your cheeks are all warm,
Your nose is all warm,
Your forehead is all warm,
Your eyes are all warm.

Your right foot is all heavy,
Your right calf is all heavy,
Your right knee is all heavy,
Your right thigh is all heavy;

Your left foot is all heavy,
Your left calf is all heavy,
Your left knee is all heavy,
Your left thigh is all heavy;

Your buttocks are all heavy,
Your abdomen is all heavy,
Your belly is all heavy,
Your chest is all heavy,
Your lower back is all heavy,
Your upper back is all heavy,
Your shoulders are all heavy;

Your right hand is all heavy,
Your right forearm is all heavy,
Your right elbow is all heavy,
Your right upper arm is all heavy;

Your left hand is all heavy,
Your left forearm is all heavy,
Your left elbow is all heavy,
Your left upper arm is all heavy;

Your neck is all heavy,
Your throat is all heavy,
Your neck is all heavy,
The back of your head is all heavy,
The top of your head is all heavy,
Your ears are all heavy,
Your lower jaw is all heavy,
Your upper jaw is all heavy,
Your cheeks are all heavy,
Your nose is all heavy,
Your forehead is all heavy,
Your eyes are all heavy.

Your right foot is all tired,
Your right calf is all tired,
Your right knee is all tired,
Your right thigh is all tired;

Your left foot is all tired,
Your left calf is all tired,
Your left knee is all tired,
Your left thigh is all tired;

Your buttocks are all tired,
Your abdomen is all tired,
Your belly is all tired,
Your chest is all tired,
Your lower back is all tired,
Your upper back is all tired,
Your shoulders are all tired;

Your right hand is all tired,
Your right forearm is all tired,
Your right elbow is all tired,
Your right upper arm is all tired;

Your left hand is all tired,
Your left forearm is all tired,
Your left elbow is all tired,
Your left upper arm is all tired;

Your neck is all tired,
Your throat is all tired,
Your neck is all tired,
The back of your head is all tired,
The top of your head is all tired,
Your ears are all tired,
Your lower jaw is all tired,
Your upper jaw is all tired,
Your cheeks are all tired,
Your nose is all tired,
Your forehead is all tired,
Your eyes are all tired.

You are tired, very tired,
You're asleep, you're sound asleep,
You're sleeping, you're sleeping soundly,
You're sleeping, you're sleeping soundly,
You hear my words,
You're sleeping, You're sleeping soundly,
You're sleeping, You're sleeping soundly,
You're sleeping, You're sleeping soundly,
You hear my words,
You answer me when I ask you something,
You're asleep, you're fast asleep..."

You can experiment with your own voice when hypnotizing. A somewhat deeper, calm and "soporific" voice, which has hardly any fluctuations in pitch and intonation, but is rather monotonous, is decidedly conducive. However, the voice should not be indifferent or harsh, but rather gentle and soothing and confidence-inspiring – after all, the other person should fall asleep …

The voice pitch that works best for oneself will be found out by some practice.

II 3. The "path" of hypnosis

The four hypnosis levels "relaxed, heavy, warm, tired" result from the structure of the human being. They are also found in three other changes in consciousness: relaxation, kundalini awakening, and learning astral projection.

The following comparison of these four processes makes it a little clearer what actually happens during hypnosis:

- In hypnosis, the hypnotist turns off the hypnotized person's waking consciousness – which means that the hypnotized person enters the dream state.

- During relaxation, the muscles are relaxed and the waking consciousness gradually turns away from the body – it turns from the outside to the inside.

- During the awakening of the Kundalini, first a relaxation occurs – depending on the method used, through the meditation, through the imagination, the mantras or the letter exercises. This is followed by a relaxation, a certain heaviness in the body. Finally, the root chakra or solar plexus becomes warm (the chakra depends on the method used). If one stays with the warmth sensation, the chakra in question eventually becomes hotter and hotter until finally the kundalini rises from that chakra.

- In many methods of learning astral projection, one first relaxes the body; then it becomes heavy and one feels it less and less; next one is filled with a pleasant warmth; thereupon the body begins to vibrate in a pleasant way at about 6Hz; finally the limbs seem to twitch, although one lies there still, and the whole body seems to rock as if in a high swell; then at the end the astral body detaches from the physical body and floats above it.

(The terms "astral body" and "life-force body" both refer to the same thing in this book – they are traditionally used in different contexts. For example, one speaks of "astral projection" and not of "life force body projection", but on the other hand of "life force" and not of "astral substance").

What the four words "relaxed, heavy, warm, tired" describe is the shifting of the focus of consciousness from the physical body to the astral body, that is, to the life force in one's body.

Tiredness appears in this list because during sleep one dissolves the waking consciousness – and tiredness leads to relaxations and sleep. During sleep, the consciousness withdraws into the life-force body (astral body) and with it steps out of the physical body a bit. This all-night, but mostly unconscious astral projection can be experienced as a flight dream.

If the waking consciousness remains intact during the shift of perception from the outside to the inside and does not dissolve, i.e. if one does not fall asleep after the relaxation, heaviness and warmth, one begins to perceive the life force body even more clearly: a vibration with 6Hz.

However, since in hypnotizing one wants to eliminate the waking consciousness of the other, one uses as the fourth "magic word" the adjective "tired" and not the verb "vibrate", which would keep the subject awake.

In the awakening of Kundalini, one also first becomes gradually more and more aware of the life force in one's own body – after all, Kundalini is a part of the life force cycle in the life force body. The three phases "relaxed, heavy, warm" also occur when learning astral projection.

However, while in astral projection one concentrates on the astral body as a whole after "warm", because one wants to detach it from the physical body, in awakening Kundalini one directs one's attention to the inside of the life force body. While one proceeds from "warm" to "vibrate" when learning astral travel, one increases the "warm" to a "hot" when awakening Kundalini.

If one is aware of these connections, one can also choose improvised words that fit the momentary situation when hypnotizing.

These processes and their relationships to each other will probably be easier to grasp with the help of a diagram:

Hypnosis and related processes			
Hypnosis	*Astral projection*	*Awakening of the Kundalini*	
↑ tired	↑ vibrate	hot ↑	↑
↑	↑ -- ↑	↑	Approach to the subconsciousness (dream state) = gradual awareness of the astral body
	↑ warm		
	↑ heavy		↑
	↑ relaxed		
waking state			

II 4. Hypnosis by gestures

The "classic gesture" in hypnosis is the pendulum. This can be some shiny or sparkling object on a string – something plain made of metal, glass, crystal, or the like. However, what is hanging at the bottom of this string should not distract or lead astray the person being hypnotized. It can be a spoon or a key on a string if need be – but not necessarily something that would occupy the other person too much such as a statuette or anything unpleasant. Something relatively neutral that attracts attention through light effects is most appropriate.

The pendulum is held at a distance of about 30-40cm in front of the head of the person who is to be hypnotized. What hangs at the bottom of the pendulum should be at the eye level of this person. The length of the string should be about 30cm, as this gives a comfortable speed of swinging of the pendulum.

The person to be hypnotized looks at the swinging pendulum. The hypnotist can speak suitable words or concentrate silently on the fact that his counterpart sees only the pendulum and that this steady movement gradually puts him to sleep.

The words that may be used should suggest a gradual falling asleep. The following is just one possibility, which can be varied:

> *"You see the pendulum ...*
> *You follow the pendulum with your eyes ...*
> *back and forth ...*
> *back and forth ...*
> *You see only the pendulum ...*
> *You are completely relaxed ...*
> *completely relaxed ...*
> *You are getting heavy ...*
> *Your eyelids are getting heavy ...*
> *Your eyelids are dropping ...*
> *Your eyelids are very heavy ...*
> *You are tired ...*
> *very tired...*
> *You are sleeping ...*
> *You are fast asleep ...*
> *deeply and soundly ..."*

The individual phases should, of course, be consistent with the subject – for example, one continues with the suggestion "Your eyelids become heavy, your eyelids fall shut" as long as the subject has not yet closed his eyes.

The word "deep" also belongs to the "hypnosis magic words". It seems to be associated with sleep – indeed, one says "deep sleep". This "deep" seems to suggest the detachment of the astral body from the physical body – possibly a "sinking down".

II 5. Hypnosis by life force

Anton Mesmer, who began to use hypnotic states for healing purposes around 1780, found out through his experiments that a person can also be hypnotized by directly affecting his life force.

Mesmer hypnosis by influencing the life force is also called "animal magnetism" in older books because Mesmer assumed that the life force was a biological variant of magnetism.

17

The method commonly used today for Mesmer hypnosis is stroking with the hand a hand's breadth above the physical body – i.e., movements within the life force body, which is just under an arm's length around the physical body.

In doing so, one may perceive the life force of the hypnotized as a warmth, a slight electric tingle, or a slight pressure. This perception of the other person's life force body is more noticeable when the other person is in an "excited state" – e.g., through violent emotions, sports, or dancing. Then you can feel the "aura" of the other person with your whole own body, if you come at least about 40-50cm close to him.

To put someone into hypnosis in the Mesmer way, you stroke with both hands about 10cm above the body along "through the air", i.e. through the life force body of the person who is in front of you – you do not touch the body of the other person. This stroking proceeds as follows:

- One strokes with both hands from the head of the lying person over his neck, the chest, the belly and then further over the legs to the feet.

- Then you shake out your hands above the head – as if you wanted to get rid of some drops of water.

- Next, starting from the head of the person lying on the ground, one strokes with both hands over his neck and then further along his arms to his hands.

- Then again shake out the hands above the head – as if to get rid of drops of water.

These four movements are repeated for a while. The first effect here is usually that the person who has been hypnotized in this way can no longer move and at first often can only speak with difficulty. Through the Mesmer method one reaches the state of relaxation and heaviness, which is often deeper than with the words and pendulum method.

Sometimes, however, a "normal hypnotic state" occurs even with the Mesmer Method.

These movements through the life force body probably cause sleep because they push the life force against the direction in which it normally flows – as described, for example, in Chinese medicine in relation to the acupuncture meridians.

II 6.   Hypnosis by Telepathy

Finally, there is remote hypnosis, which is caused by telepathy. Here the hypnotist takes control of the hypnotized person, although the latter is not physically present at all.

How the hypnotist does it and what tools he uses depends on the hypnotist's view of the world and the reason for the remote hypnosis.

If the hypnotist has already performed a demon summoning ("evocation"), he can perform the remote hypnosis like such a summoning. The usual method would be to set up a protective circle, e.g. with the help of the small pentagram ritual, in front of which there is a triangle into which the person to be hypnotized is called. This procedure leads quite surely to the fact that the called person has a "mental blackout", i.e. that his waking consciousness is interrupted – similarly as with a "film tear" after too much alcohol.

You can also choose another arrangement for remote hypnosis if you are not familiar with evocations. For example, you can sit down on the carpet and imagine that you summon the other person and he sits or lies down on the carpet in front of you. In this method, too, one should speak very firmly and command the other person to come here right now.

If the hypnotist has the goal that the hypnotized person does something specific, the central part of remote hypnosis is the vivid imagination of the action in question – after the hypnotist has inwardly, i.e. telepathically established contact with the person who is to be hypnotized.

Remote hypnosis contains an obvious risk: if it succeeds and the subject really falls into hypnosis, he is no longer fully sane – which can have disastrous effects if, for example, the subject is currently driving his car on the highway. One should therefore plan remote hypnosis experiments very carefully and make sure that the person who is to be hypnotized is at home and is not working with a circular saw or the like.

In general, remote hypnosis that has not been agreed upon with the hypnotized person can be counted as "dark gray to black magic", since it massively interferes with the will of another person, and the hypnotized person may be in danger, because due to his hypnotic state he can no longer perceive his situation with his waking consciousness and behave in a reasonable way.

When I once carried out such experiments with my "magic teacher" Axel, Axel thought to himself on the arranged evening that it can't come to anything and went to the next pub to have a drink.

The other guests in the pub then told him the next day that he suddenly, although he was still almost sober by his standards, put his glass down on an imaginary table and left the pub. Apparently he managed to get home safely through the traffic and lay down in his bed, where he then awoke the next morning fully clothed.

Axel has thus been in a form of hypnosis in which he has had no memory at all, but apparently had still had such routine behaviors as obeying traffic rules available to him.

The extent to which a hypnotized person can still have his normal everyday abilities during hypnosis varies from person to person.

III Possible Applications

Of course, there is also the question of why one would want to hypnotize someone – except just to research hypnotizing …

III 1. Research of the Psyche

The most obvious application of hypnosis is the research of the psyche, because during hypnosis the hypnotist has a direct contact with the subconsciousness of the hypnotized.

In this research with the help of hypnosis one can distinguish two aspects:

On the one hand, forgotten memories and repressed experiences of the hypnotized person and the like can be made conscious again through hypnosis. As a rule, however, after awakening from hypnosis, the hypnotized person knows nothing of what he or she has told the hypnotist. In order to use the information obtained through hypnosis, it must be told to the subject by the hypnotist.

It is also possible to record what the hypnotized person tells the hypnotist and then play it back to the subject – this has the advantage that the subject really hears verbatim what he has said and does not have to believe what the hypnotist tells him. This makes it easier to integrate the information obtained in this way.

Of course, the real work for the hypnotized person begins after hypnosis. It consists of finding the corresponding feelings, memories, etc. in himself again and being able to look at them consciously, then taking the time to really feel them and then finally embracing them, i.e. integrating them into one's own psyche again.

Secondly, the hypnotist will learn much about the structure of the psyche, the nature of consciousness, and the inner structures and dynamics of the human being through his experiences with the hypnotized and what they say and do under hypnosis.

I myself have gained a large part of the basis of my own knowledge about the psyche through about 50 hypnosis experiments. This direct contact with the subconscious of another person is extremely vivid and helpful … Afterwards the word "subconsciousness" is clearly more than just an intellectual concept.

III 2.   Healing of the psyche

The psyche can also be healed under hypnosis. In most cases suggestions are used for this purpose. For example, it is suggested to the subject that he is no longer afraid of flying.

Probably this procedure should not be called "healing", but rather "reprogramming" – where not even the old "program" is deleted, but only overwritten with a new "program".

This form of healing is clearly not directed at the actual roots of the problem. Therefore, one should not use it as the central cure, but rather as an auxiliary measure.

In contrast to the use of suggestions in hypnosis, finding the causes of diseases or mental disorders with the help of hypnosis is a method that looks much deeper into the psyche and therefore can have a deeper and more thorough effect.

In the case of major disorders such as alcoholism, suggestions under hypnosis are not effective enough to cure the problem.

III 3.   Healing of the body

Just as psychological problems can be partially "cured" or more precisely "eliminated" by suggestions, physical problems such as smoking, sleep disorders, neurodermatitis, and the like can also be cured or at least suppressed by suggestions.

Here, too, it is more promising to find the actual causes of the illnesses with the help of hypnosis than to cure them with the help of suggestions under hypnosis.

III 4.   Solving crimes etc.

Another possibility is the criminalistic use of hypnosis. In this case, both the victim and the suspect or perpetrator can be hypnotized in order to obtain new information from them. However, this procedure is quite questionable from a legal point of view, as it interferes with the self-determination of the hypnotized person if the hypnosis is not voluntary.

In any case, the information obtained in this way must be verified again, since it comes from the subconscious mind, which follows the "dream logic" and not the usual logic of the waking state. Information and confessions obtained in this way are also very doubtful because the hypnotized are not fully conscious and therefore not capable of judgment in the usual sense.

III 5. Research of previous incarnations

Hypnosis and hypnosis-like states such as deep relaxation are also used to research past lives. However, this is a procedure fraught with some uncertainties – how will one know the manner in which the information obtained through such a "regression" came about?

There are at least three different possible explanations for the origin of the images and the like that appear during a regression:

> - Contents of the subconscious are narrated in hypnosis in dramatic form. For example, a fear of dogs together with all associations connected with this fear can be condensed into a story about a terrible experience with dogs.
> This story then explains very conclusively all aspects of the person's fear of dogs – simply because this story arose from the person's fear of dogs.

> - The second possibility is the telepathic acquisition of information. Thus the person concerned can (of course unconsciously) build elements into his story, of which he cannot know anything and which can be checked afterwards. This can be e.g. the exact ground plan of a church in a place, in which the concerning person never has been, or an object, which lies buried at a certain place or the like.
> For the time being only the telepathy itself can be proved by such information. Whether the story, in which the possibly only telepathically acquired information was built in, is a memory of a former life or a "dramatized fear", remains unclear for the time being.

> - The third possibility is that the story told under hypnosis is actually the memories of a past life.
> Deciding which of these three possibilities applies in a particular case is not easy. This verification of the results of a regression is also beyond the scope of this book (if needed, see my book "Reinkarnation").

However, the story obtained through hypnosis or regression may be of great use if it actually contains an intense feeling or even a trauma, since one can then use this story as a starting point for resolving this feeling or healing this trauma. It does not matter whether the story arose from the trauma or whether this story is the memory of a past life – the way of healing this trauma remains the same.

The first step in this process is to look at these feelings and find associations to this story, gradually creating a clearer picture of the feelings in this story (and therefore in the person himself). This gives the story more contour and clarity, and its place in the person's psyche becomes clearer.

The second step is the conscious experience of these emotions, i.e. the "feeling of the emotions". In this way the person gains contact with the emotions in this story. The emotions can begin to move and flow again – they become free again.

The third step is to embrace this story or the figure of the hypnotized in this story, if he appears in the story itself (which is very likely). Through this embracing of the story, the feelings or the self-image in this story, the isolation of these feelings from the rest of the psyche is removed and these feelings can be reintegrated.

III 6.   Exploration of magical possibilities

One can also use hypnosis to explore magical possibilities and make things happen in a magical way. Around 1950, this arrangement was often called "magician and medium," where the magician has usually been a dominant male and the medium a more passive female.

The procedure is always the same in this application of hypnosis: the magician hypnotizes the medium and then has the medium either telepathically obtain information or telekinetically exert an effect. So the "magician and medium" procedure served a more effective exercise of telepathy and telekinesis.

These two abilities, i.e. telepathy and telekinesis, are located in the life force body (astral body) and thus lie in the subconsciousness. Therefore, in order to exercise them, one must either make contact with one's subconscious mind (as is common today) or put someone else into a subconscious state and then direct them – that is, hypnotize someone.

This method can be used to find a missing person, to discover a missing piece of information, etc., that is, to help when normal methods fail.

Of course, this method can also be used when you want to do something that is illegal – then you would be in the realm of black magic. You can use the "magician and medium" method to spy out inaccessible places, explore security precautions and the like. The worst thing would be to interfere by this method with the consiousness of a person who ist driving a car – the real cause of the following accident thus brought about would never be discoverd.

The medium is put into hypnosis by the magician and then sent (internally/tele-pathically) to the place in question, whereupon the hypnotized medium can describe the place and the things in it. Reading texts with the help of this method seems to be rather difficult – grasping pictures is telepathically apparently easier than grasping letters and numbers.

However, information obtained in this way is sometimes somewhat fuzzy, so one should be careful about drawing conclusions from it. Possibly this fuzziness is due to the fact that by telepathy or on an astral journey one has a somewhat different perception, in which the contours are sometimes slightly blurred and the scenery sometimes appears as if shrouded in a light fog. Also, not all details are always seen as in normal optical perception.

When using telekinesis by a medium, it is of course a question of what one intends to do with it. Does one want to help someone or harm someone? Or does one even want to kill somebody by a car-crash?

Here the door is wide open to black magic. Fortunately, with the "magician and medium" procedure, as with all methods, it is not so easy to achieve a great effect – without talent and practice and a great motivation there does not happen much … Therefore, abuse of this method is not as simple as it may seem at first.

In all processes under hypnosis it makes sense to use the images in the hypnotized person instead of working against them – this is also true for "magician and medium" magic. For example, if the hypnotized person has Mars at his ascendant and is therefore a warlike type, one should use sexual or warlike images for all suggestions – this works best …

If one wants to help another in this way and this other person is, for example, firmly anchored in the Christian faith, one should use Christian images for this help, because the person concerned can most easily understand, accept and integrate these images.

These principles also apply when one wants to harm another via the "magician and medium" method.

A somewhat devious method is to suggest a false image to a hypnotized person, on the basis of which he then does from his own motivation what the magician actually wants from him – e.g. because the hypnotized person suddenly thinks a person is an attacker who threatens the daughter of the hypnotized person.

Here a possibly existing dark creativity has many possibilities of design, the effect of which is fortunately limited by the fact that it is not as easy to implement effectively images in the psyche of another person as it sounds at first. But it's possible and this method is still being used today …

III 7. Commanding actions

The "classic case" and the most spectacular performance of hypnosis is the "hypnotic command" to a person, which the latter then carries out either immediately or later, without consciously wanting to do so. It is obvious that in this way one can do a lot of harm or even make people commit crimes they do not want to commit.

Again, you cannot command anything against the images in the subject's psyche, but you can use the images in the subject's psyche in such a way that when he carries out the hypnotic command, he believes, for example, that he is defending himself, when in fact he is attacking the other person. It is obvious that this is an area that belongs to black magic.

Fortunately, even this procedure is not as easy to implement as it seems at first. For one thing, the subject must first agree to his hypnosis – hypnotizing someone unnoticed is anything but easy, even though it is quite possible. On the other hand, the hypnotist must also have the necessary determination and strength in his hypnosis to implement the hypnotic command.

This procedure has become famous through the "Harry Potter" novels. The spell belonging to it is "Imperio!".

This procedure will be described in more detail in a later chapter.

A second spectacular use of hypnosis is that the hypnotist can often make a hypnotized person do things that he would not normally be able to do, especially physically. This can involve his sense of balance, dexterity, as well as strength.

These abilities are similar to the amazing abilities displayed in some martial arts such as karate. The reason for this is quite simple:

- The karateka is one-pointed when he smashes a brick with the edge of his hand.

He also has an internal image of hitting a place below the brick with his hand, largely ignoring the brick.

- The hypnotized person follows the hypnotist's command in a one-directed manner, whereby his "switched off" waking consciousness cannot cast any doubt into his one-directedness.

The hypnotist sends to the hypnotized, both by his command and by his imagination, the image of the accomplished task: "You will now break this brick."

This single-mindedness and this imagination of the accomplished task can be obtained both by independent and conscious concentration and by being hypnotized.

The hypnotist, by the way, needs exactly the same two abilities to be able to hypnotize: single-mindedness and the vividly intense imagination of the accomplished act.

"Concentration and imagination" are generally the two pillars on which effective magic is based …

IV   The Depth of the Hypnotic State

Hypnosis consists in the fact that the focus of the hypnotized person gradually shifts from the waking consciousness to the subconsciousness and, consequently, from the external world to his life force body. Therefore, the depth of a hypnosis can vary – depending on how far the focus of the hypnotized person is shifted towards the subconsciousness, i.e. to his life force body, on this path.

The stages on this path are:

- Starting point: waking consciousness/outside world.

- 1st step: **listening** and watching the hypnotist (word, pendulum, and gestures)

- 2nd step: **relax**

- 3rd step: the attention of the person to be hypnotized is focussed completely on the hypnotist → narrowing of waking consciousness and therefore **fixation** on the hypnotist

- 4th step: the body becomes **heavy** → unable to move, rigidity of the body, "petrification" (the control of the body is stopped as if in sleep)

- 5th step: the body is already motionless or immobile and now becomes additionally **warm** (this warmth is the perception of one's own life force body).

- 6th step: the waking consciousness becomes blurred, i.e. one becomes **tired** (the hypnotized person approaches the sleep state – however, during hypnosis a connection to the hypnotist remains)

- 7th step: the waking consciousness dissolves and one enters a **"waking sleep"**, i.e. the hypnotic state

- 8th step: the **life force body** begins to vibrate with approx. 6Hz (this is the second perception of the life force body after the warmth)

28

- 9th step: possibly the process is continued, whereby one either awakens one's own **Kundalini** (the warmth becomes heat) or an **astral projection** begins (the astral body detaches as a whole from the physical body)

- End point: hypnosis (dream state / astral projection)

The desired depth of the hypnotic state depends on what one wants to achieve with this state. Usually, reaching "waking sleep" is the goal, as the hypnotist can then talk to the hypnotized person. In this state, the hypnotist can question the hypnotized and get answers directly from his subconscious or telepathically obtained information. In addition, the hypnotist can also give orders ("hypnotic commands") to the hypnotized in this state.

V Awakening from Hypnosis

Waking up from hypnosis is in most cases easier than putting the subject into hypnosis. Here, too, the will of the hypnotist is the essential element.

V 1. Awakening by words

It is possible to awaken the hypnotized person with a formula that reverses the sequence of "magic words" used in hypnosis, transforming them into their counterparts:

"You have now slept for a while,
You are now waking up again,
You are now returning from sleep,
You feel fresh,
You feel light,
You feel like moving,
You are awake and alert..."

One has to see in the concrete case if this short formula is sufficient – maybe one has to extend it a bit, so that the person concerned has time to "wake up", i.e. to return from the hypnotic state.

There seems to be nothing after hypnosis that would correspond to "morning tiredness" – the hypnotized are "really awake" again immediately after returning from hypnosis.

The four important "magic words" in hypnotizing and in awakening from hypnosis are:

the "magic words" on the "hypnosis way"			
Waking state			
↓	relaxed	lively	↑
↓	heavy	light	↑
↓	warm	refreshed	↑
↓	tired	awake	↑
Hypnosis state			

Waking from hypnosis is sometimes also done by a simple clapping with the hands – but this works well only if either the hypnosis has not been very deep or if the magician and the medium are well attuned to each other, and the clapping as a wake-up signal is well anchored in the medium's psyche by constant use in this function.

It seems as if hypnosis can be dissolved most easily in the same or a similar way as it was produced before – which is quite plausible.

However, hypnotic states can also dissolve by themselves after a while.

V 2. Awakening by life force

The Mesmer method of awakening is as follows:

- One strokes with both hands from the two feet of the lying person along over his legs and then further over the belly, the chest and the neck up to the head.

- Then you shake out your hands above the head – as if you wanted to get rid of some drops of water.

- Next, from the two hands of the lying person, one strokes along his arms and then further over the belly, the chest, the neck up to the head.

- Then again shake out the hands above the head – a s if to get rid of some drops of water.

31

The movements in waking according to the Mesmer method are exactly the opposite of those in hypnotizing according to this method.

V 3.   Independent awakening

The independent awakening of the hypnotized person seems to occur only rarely – I have not experienced it in my own hypnosis experiments.

The recognition of his condition by the hypnotized himself, whereby he then begins to resist his hypnosis, seems to occur only when the hypnotist is so clumsy as to command the hypnotized to do something that contradicts his world view or his values. Such a command creates an inner contradiction in the hypnotized person, which can wake him up from hypnotic sleep, whereupon the hypnotist loses control over him.

Such a resistance is described very vividly in the "Harry Potter" books, where Harry is able to resist the "Imperio!" command from Professor Moody and also from Voldemort.

VI   The Side Effects of Hypnotizing

An important point to consider is the effect of hypnosis on the hypnotized – and, of course, on the hypnotist.

In this chapter we are not concerned with the effects that hypnosis is intended for and can achieve, such as healing of the psyche or body, regression and telepathic information retrieval, but with the "side effects" of hypnosis.

VI 1.   One-time hypnosis

A one-time hypnosis will hardly have a lasting side effect – both the hypnotist and the hypnotized person experience first of all that hypnosis is possible and what this state looks like.

VI 2.   Frequent hypnosis

Frequent hypnosis experiments with the same person, however, have a rather distinct side effect: a tendency to disintegrate the psyche – which is not a desirable effect.

This side effect comes about in a rather simple way: when talking to a hypnotized person, one has as interlocutor not the waking consciousness of the subject, but a part of his subconsciousness. If one visits this part frequently during hypnosis, this part develops a greater independence and begins to grow and develop into a greater independence. This greater independence may cause that part of the psyche to be more difficult to integrate into the psyche afterwards.

There is also a second effect: The hypnotist becomes more and more dominant and the hypnotized more and more subordinate by frequent hypnotizing. Even if you have two independent people in the beginning, the "classical" role distribution of "magician and medium" can form through frequent hypnotizing. This need not happen, but the danger is great.

VI 3. Alternatives to Hypnosis

Fortunately, there are some alternatives to hypnosis: dream journeys, auto-suggestions ("self-hypnosis") and meditation.

These methods are based on the fact that a person is able to consciously go into his subconscious, i.e. he learns to be in his waking consciousness and in his dream state (subconscious) at the same time. This is not as exotic as it may sound – almost everyone knows this state:

> - When you wake up from a dream in the morning, you sometimes continue dreaming for another 5-10 seconds, i.e. the dream continues to run in its own dynamics, although you are already awake – this is then roughly as if you were watching a movie.
> Here the dream consciousness has been supplemented by the waking consciousness.

> - When you are sitting in a train and looking out of the window, you sometimes get into a vivid daydream and find yourself on vacation by the sea and even feel the sand under your bare feet. Then you suddenly "wake up" from the daydream and see that you are sitting on the train instead.
> Here the waking consciousness has been supplemented by the dream consciousness.

One can learn to get into this state on purpose and on a certain subject ("dream journey") and then one can also experience everything that one could experience with the help of hypnosis.

During autosuggestion, one first puts oneself into the deepest possible relaxation, i.e. one goes with one's consciousness a little way from the outside to the inside, from the waking consciousness to the dream consciousness, from the physical body to the astral body.

Then one speaks inwardly the sentence that expresses what one wants to achieve. This can be anything: "I am popular.", "I am rich.", "I am strong." etc. These sentences can also refer to something more concrete like: "I pass my high school graduation with a grade of 'A'.", "I find a good and cheap apartment." or "I find my dream man this month."

You can either say this sentence once with a lot of emphasis during autosuggestion or speak it inwardly very often like a mantra.

Meditation is a more general alternative to hypnosis because meditation offers different ways of coordinating consciousness. The three main forms of meditation are:

- waking consciousness + subconsciousness   => dream journey
- waking consciousness + deep sleep   => silent meditation (Zen)
- waking consciousness + ecstasy state   => kundalini awakening

The dream journey, autosuggestion and meditation have the great advantage of integrating the psyche and promoting self-determination – simply because one's waking consciousness makes contact with the various parts or states of consciousness. This contact is the basis for integration.

VII Experiences with Hypnosis

Under hypnosis, especially those parts of the psyche that are under great emotional pressure emerge. These are the same parts of the psyche that come to the surface in dreams and in dream journeys.

Therefore, if the hypnotized person has within him violent feelings or even unhealed traumas, the scenes and stories that appear under hypnosis can be quite violent. Therefore, the hypnotist also needs a certain "emotional steadiness" to be able to deal in a reasonable way with these scenes that the hypnotized experiences and describes.

Under hypnosis, events can also occur that the hypnotized person did not experience himself, but his ancestors did. This "preservation of family history" is also an important element in family constellations, where it becomes very clear that people can also carry feelings and behaviors of their parents, grandparents, great-grandparents, etc. within themselves.

Due to these "inherited memories" also rapes, war experiences, earthquakes and the like can appear under hypnosis, which the hypnotized person has not experienced himself. At this point at the latest, the hypnotist needs a minimum of psychological sensitivity and skill …

But of course it does not always have to be so violent. There are also hypnoses in which the hypnotized person responds, but nothing spectacular or even interesting happens.

I myself learned hypnosis through Axel Büdenbender – a magic adventurer who had taken me on as a "sorcerer's apprentice" and whose maxim is "The important thing is that it cracks and makes you dizzy!"

One day he put a book in my hand and said, "Here, read pages 174 and 175 and tomorrow you'll hypnotize me."

At that time I was much too shy to say that I could not possibly hypnotize another person. So I read through the two pages, memorized the instructions, and tried hypnotizing Axel the next night. To my great astonishment, it worked on the third try.

Since Axel, as I said, is an adventurer, the scenes I experienced with him in his hypnotized state were sometimes quite adventurous.

For example, Axel once started talking under hypnosis to someone he apparently saw himself talking to. After a few sentences I realized that Axel had just been offered a job as a guard at the Gates of Hell by his counterpart.

It was not so easy to interfere in the conversation (of which I could only hear Axel's part) and to dissuade Axel from accepting this job …

Of course I don't know what would have happened if he had accepted this offer, and if anything would have happened at all, but I was quite happy that I could stop him and bring him back from hypnosis.

In another hypnosis session, Axel seemed to be in a past life and experienced being tried as a witch in a court of law and eventually burned at the stake – that was pretty intense!

That was during one of the first hypnosis attempts. I chose at that time to let Axel finish experiencing and telling this story, because I thought that this information might be helpful to Axel.

Afterwards, we had a long discussion about whether these images were from a past life or whether they were a dramatization of his conflicts with authority and his fear of fire.

During another hypnosis session, a completely different personality suddenly emerged in Axel: Axel grinned, changed his facial expressions, and drew a spell circle

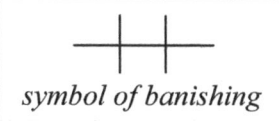

symbol of banishing

around himself with the help of symbols I had never seen before – once each in each cardinal direction, the symbol shown on the left. There he was, sitting on his chair, grinning maliciously and challengingly – this was the most stable spell circle I had seen up to that point.

I tried to break this circle to regain contact to Axel and regain hypnotic control over him, but it wasn't that easy. Only when I called glistening white light from above (from Kether) into Axel's crown chakra and then into his whole body, causing this other personality to fade, was I able to break the spell circle and bring Axel back from hypnosis.

When the light filled Axel, his facial expressions relaxed and he slumped a little – as if he had fallen asleep.

One can of course wonder if a demon has taken possession of Axel, especially since calling the "God-Light" (Kether) is an exorcism method. This is again one of the points which are very difficult to decide – accordingly long Axel and I discussed about it afterwards.

Axel could also have had "demon pictures" in himself (which will have been the case for sure) and dramatized his general attitude towards authorities in this picture of the described banishing circle scene. However, if he carries these images within himself, they would also be a suitable point for real demons to dock.

On the other hand, one can also argue that if a real demon has made contact with Axel, Axel would develop demon images in himself.

However, since these demon images can be explained well from his biography (counter-reaction to his time in a convent school), the model of "dramatization of contents of the subconscious" (as in a dream) seems to me to be more plausible.

In case of doubt it always makes sense to use the simplest explanation – this proves to be the right one in almost all cases.

When Axel once again assumed a different personality in a hypnosis and refused to come back out of hypnosis, I tried various unorthodox wake-up methods such as pouring a glass of water in his face, but this was completely ineffective – bringing him back is not that easy either when the hypnotized person is in an independent state not induced by the hypnotist and this state has stabilized (such as with the spell circle).

Of course, the hypnotic experiences do not always have to be as violent and tend to be as dark as in the scenes described here – this corresponds to Axel's inner imagery.

I have also hypnotized other people who, for example, met their power animal in the process or simply entered a very deep relaxation in which they could no longer move.

This kind of experience is especially instructive for the hypnotist – where else can you communicate with the subconsciousness of another person in such a direct way? And where else can you learn to deal with spells, demons, etc. "by the way", so to speak?

VIII   Hypnosis-like Processes

There are some processes that are very similar to hypnosis, since changes in the usual order of consciousness and body also take place.

VIII 1.   Transference of consciousness

During healings, there is the possibility that the healer transfers his consciousness into the sick person and looks at the organs, the chakras and the psyche of the person in a very direct way.

In terms of extending one's consciousness to another, this form of diagnosis is very similar to hypnosis. However, the consciousness of the sick person is not eliminated – the sick person can sometimes feel the presence of the healer's consciousness in his body.

The procedure is quite simple, although it may require some practice by the healer: The healer focuses his attention on the patient, gropes inwardly for the patient's body, and imagines his consciousness shifting into the sick person's body.

It is helpful, of course, if the healer has first practiced this looking at the inside of the body, the chakras and the psyche on himself, otherwise he would have to learn two things at once: the shifting of consciousness into another body and the looking at the inside of the body.

This process sounds much less spectacular if it is understood as a systematic form of telepathy, in which not only a single detail, but the entire body of another person is grasped.

As with most things, this form of transmission of consciousness can only be truly understood and appreciated once one has performed it oneself. It is an extremely useful diagnostic method.

It can also be used for therapy, which obviously requires a transition from telepathy to telekinesis – this transition, however, is very inconspicuous when performed. After all, it is not a long way from the perception of one's own hand to the movement of one's own hand …

One can, if one is with his consciousness in the other person, change the pictures in the psyche of the other person – which of course should always happen only in consultation with the person concerned. In doing so, one can, for example, heal images of inner wounds or, in the case of someone who immediately falls into actionism at the slightest disturbance, ask Buddha Amitabha into the root of the third eye (approximately at the pituitary gland).

There is also the possibility of changing the life force distribution in the chakras, as there are often one-sidednesses and polarizations in them, which also correspond to one-sided and polarized psychic states, such as a perpetrator/victim polarization. This particular polarization is found in the Third Eye and the Hara.

This method of directing the life force is also suitable, for example, for calming a panic attack. In this case, there is a life force congestion in the Third Eye and a life force deficiency in the Hara – the panic attack is the symptom of a victim. Therefore, directing the life force from the Third Eye to the Hara calms the panic-attack. Moving the life force is done by imagining that the life force flows from the Third Eye to the Hara. This is easier when you are with your consciousness in the body of the other person who has this panic attack.

One can, when one is with one's consciousness in the body of another person, also look directly at their feelings, although it generally seems easier to look at the chakras and then do something about the feelings and images in them.

Contact with the organs is somewhat different than contact with the chakras: The organs are much more direct and emotional than the chakras, and often a bit naughty – they are downright fun to talk to! Since they are physical and not made of life force like the chakras, influencing the organs is more difficult.

However, one should be cautious whenever influencing another person. One should acquire some expertise about the chakras, the emotions and the organs before changing anything about them.

VIII 2. Darshan

A process quite similar to the transference of consciousness in healing is darshan. In this process, a disciple sits before a master ("guru") and inwardly opens himself to the master. The master, in turn, extends his own consciousness to the disciple, drawing him into the same state of consciousness as that in which the teacher is.

Probably the easiest way to illustrate this is with an example: When I was in my early 20s, I once went to a lecture by the "Ananda Marga" people, which took place in an adjoining room of a vegetarian restaurant. There were about a dozen of us, along with the yogi who gave the talk. After the lecture, we exchanged anecdotes and then meditated.

During this round of meditation, I suddenly felt the yogi's consciousness within me and experienced how he, as it were, gently stroked my thoughts with his hand, whereupon they fell silent. Since then, at any time, within a second, I can change into this state of silence, where only the consciousness itself is there, aware of itself –

without thoughts, feelings and perceptions.

That was a very great gift!

This form of expansion of consciousness is also found in consecrations, where the magician or priest expands his consciousness to the object to be consecrated and then "imprints" this object with his intention and with the images expressing this intention.

A special and comprehensive form of such consecration is energetic Feng Shui, in which the entire life force of a room, apartment or other place is dissolved and redesigned by "imprinting" new images on the space. Afterwards, such a place feels completely different than before.

Another variant are initiations. Here, too, the person to be initiated is connected by a teacher or the like with a certain state of consciousness, which he can then experience. In many cases not only the consciousness of the leader of the initiation is extended to the initiate, because the leader of the initiation has connected himself with the consciousness of a deity before. Thus, the initiate receives contact with the deity in question.

This process may sound a bit adventurous and like marble temples, processions, ritual fires and long invocations. However, if someone is practiced in making contact with a deity and extending his consciousness to others, he can show this deity-consciousness to another person without any preparation and "special external circumstances", if the conversation should come to this subject and the other person would like to experience it.

Such an initiation is, so to speak, an invocation, which the person concerned does not carry out himself, but another person, who is practiced in making contact with deities. Basically, this is a commonly known process: every blessing given to the congregation in the church is such a connection of the congregation with God or Christ through the priest.

As always, there are different qualities (deities) with which one can be connected, and also different intensities in which this can happen.

Another form of such an initiation is the common dream journey to a deity. This is a bit more elaborate, but has the advantage that the "student" is independent in this process, gets to know a path to the deity and probably sees more images connected with this deity.

The independent variant of an initiation is the invocation of a deity, in which one invokes the deity, imagines it inwardly and then identifies with it. In this way, one invokes the consciousness of this deity into oneself, so to speak. The experience of such an invocation differs of course very much from deity to deity – the mischievous Pan appears differently than the grasping Horus and also the light Apollo appears differently than the cunning Loki.

Invocation is the counterpart of hypnosis: in hypnosis the hypnotist extends his consciousness to the hypnotized – in invocation the magician invites the deity to extend its consciousness to the magician.

The principle of an "external connection" as in invocation is also found in energetic Feng Shui. Here, for example, one place of the room that one is energetically designing is connected with the elf from the oak tree in the garden in front of the house, another place is connected with the river in the valley where this house is located, and so on.

What is changed in this form of Feng Shui is the life force of a room, home or place. This is the more important part of Feng Shui – the other part is arranging furniture in a room, planting beds in a garden, etc. Since in almost all cases the house is already standing and the garden is already laid out, in the concrete activity of Feng Shui one almost always has to do with changing some small things materially and then changing the whole thing energetically, i.e. with the help of the life force.

At the end of the Feng Shui "treatment" of a place, the inner (life force) image newly created in it can be charged once again by linking the room as a whole with the glowing iron-nickel core of the earth.

A last variant is the extension of the consciousness of a deity to a human being or to a group of human beings, which at least partly also proceeds from the deity itself.

The most well-known event of this kind in our culture is probably the "Pentecostal miracle", i.e. the filling of the apostles with the Holy Spirit – thereby the consciousness of the apostles was extended to God the Father and possibly also to Christ.

VIII 3. Phowa

The Phowa is one of the "six yogas of Naropa". Naropa was a Mahasiddi ("Buddhist yogi") from northern India, whose teachings have been the main foundation of Tibetan Buddhism. He lived from 1016-1100 AD.

The Phowa is a rather adventurous sounding procedure: When a yogi is close to death, but still wants to do some things in his present life, there is the possibility that he transfers his consciousness into the body of someone who has just died and revives this body with the help of life force. Then the consciousness of this yogi lives in the revived body of the deceased.

This is probably the most extreme form of hypnosis imaginable.

VIII 4.   Possession

In a real possession, a spirit exercises hypnosis: It extends its consciousness to a human being and temporarily determines his actions or permanently takes over his body. True possessions are extremely rare, however, because there is little reason for the spirit of a dead person to take hold of a living person and try to control him or her – moreover, this spirit of the dead would have to have a high level of concentration and, ideally, some basic knowledge of magic.

The possession has similarity with the Phowa – however only in the point that both times a durable steering of a body by another consciousness is aimed at.

VIII 5.   Hypnosis-fight

The hypnosis fight can be performed as a game together with a friend. Both should have about the same amount of experience with magical and spiritual things. If possible, neither of the two should be clearly more dominant than the other.

Both sit down in front of each other at a comfortable distance and begin to concentrate on the other and wordlessly put him or her into a state of hypnosis. In the process, one will often notice what the other is imagining:

> A wraps B in his imagination in a black cloth to put him to sleep – so B imaginatively tears the black cloth apart as soon as he perceives it.

> Then B has the idea to let the life force of A flow downwards into the earth – whereupon A closes e.g. his aura by an imagined armor.

> Thereupon A goes over to the counterattack and lets the eyes of B become completely heavy – whereupon B calls glistening light into himself and lets it radiate outward through his eyes.

> Next, B imagines to let A sink into the earth – whereupon A turns into a bird or an angel.

> B doesn't let this happen just like that and clips the wings of the bird …

During this hypnosis fight both are silent – the imagined images of the other can be perceived inwardly even without words.

This friendly hypnosis fight highly promotes the perceptiveness and creativity of the two sorcerer's apprentices who carry out this experiment …

Such battles of will and imagination are found in many cultures as battles between two sorcerers, often belonging to two different religions. The two most famous magician fights are probably the one between the Tibetan yogi Milarepa and the Bön priest, and the magic fight between the prophet Elijah and the Ba'al priests in the Old Testament.

In this very pragmatic way one found out at that time whose system and above all whose God was the stronger one … and who was right consequently …

Such magician fights are also often found in fantasy novels, comics, movies etc.: the fight of the two fakirs in "Asterix and the Magic Carpet", the magician fights in the MCU movie "Dr. Strange", the fight between Master Yoda and Count Dooku in "Star Wars", the battle of wills between Gandalf and Saruman in Isengard in "The Lord of the Rings" etc.

The motif of the hypnotist-magician is obviously firmly anchored in the collective subconscious …

VIII 6.   Expansion of consciousness

Telepathy is the extension of one's own consciousness to other objects or living beings – how else could the consciousness have received the telepathically acquired information? Since there is no physical connection through which this information could have reached the person concerned, it can only have been obtained directly through the consciousness.

In hypnosis, the consciousness not only expands to an object or another person, but takes over this object or body temporarily and moves it in the same way as the consciousness can move its own body. Here the extension of consciousness can be seen even more clearly. That which is moved telekineticly has temporarily become a "second body" for the consciousness of the person exercising this telekinesis.

In hypnosis, this expansion of consciousness is clearly felt only by the hypnotist, who extends his own consciousness to the hypnotized. In remote hypnosis, on the other hand, it is obvious even to outsiders that the hypnotist has taken control of the body of the hypnotized and consequently must have extended his consciousness to the "remote hypnotized". It is interesting to note that the remotely hypnotized person is not within reach or sight, but may be several miles away – thus hypnosis is not effected by words or gestures.

There is also a combination of hypnosis and telekinesis or a mixture of both. In this case, the hypnotist, who could also be called a "magician" here, extends his consciousness to another person and moves the other person as he likes – the other person is "remotely controlled" by the hypnotist, so to speak. This method is mainly used in advanced magical fighting techniques.

In this way, the magician can prevent another person from doing something specific, such as walking towards the magician. The magician can also give another a non-contact blow only "by consciousness" or he can also make the other person think he is a dog, for example.

This "hostile takeover" of another person's body is a very advanced form of hypnosis, even though the basic principle of extending the hypnotist's consciousness to the hypnotized is the same as in simple hypnosis.

VIII 7.   Spiritus familiaris

The extension of consciousness to something outside one's own body is also found in another magical technique: in the production and use of a "spiritus familiaris" or "house spirit."

First of all, a material body is made for this spirit, which corresponds to the future task of this spirit. For a general helper and protector, for example, one can take the form of an owl or a dog – depending on whether the power of the dog or the wisdom of the owl is more important to one. If you have something specific in mind, you should thoroughly study the myths that exist about the chosen form, because ultimately it is the symbolism and not the intention that prevails.

Then one chooses a substance from which to make that shape. For most things, a sun symbolism is suitable. For this, you melt one part beeswax in a pot, add two parts yellow clay and mix both thoroughly until a homogeneous mass is formed. From this substance, one then forms the shape of the owl, the dog, etc.

In this form, while it is still warm and soft, a hole is drilled.

Then one boils a thick decoction ("very strong, almost thick tea") of chamomile flowers and adds a few drops of the homeopathic remedy Aurum chloratum C200.

If one prefers a lunar symbolism, one takes white clay and white wax (kerosene). As a liquid in this case, one uses, for example, a decoction of poppy seeds, to which one adds a few drops of Argentum nitricum C200.

The liquid prepared from the plant decoction and the homeopathic remedy is poured into the hole in the figure and a few drops of the magicians own blood are added. Then the opening of this hole is tightly closed with a ball made of the beeswax/clay mixture or, if the moon symbolism is used, of the wax/clay mixture.

After a few days the figure then becomes very hard on the one hand, but on the other hand also very elastic, so that it becomes extremely shock-resistant. It also feels very organic – almost like skin.

Now this figure gets a name and is filled with further life force. To do this, you hold it in your left hand, hold your right hand over it and imagine life force flowing out of your hand into the figure – first the element earth, then water, then air, finally fire and at the end light.

You can also use sunlight, moonlight, menstrual blood, sperm, etc. to charge the figure – it depends on the magician's style and the task of the spirit created in this way. The classic method of charging with life force is using the blood of sacrificed animals.

Charging should be repeated regularly in the first period. After some time, however, the spirit created in this way stabilizes, so that it does not harm it if you do not "feed" it for a few days.

This spirit can now be sent around and given tasks: to obtain information, to bring an object into one's own life, to arrange a meeting, to bring about a desired "coincidence", to cause harm to another person, etc. The list of possible uses of such a spirit is almost unlimited.

However, making such a spirit also has a big disadvantage: the spirit gradually becomes more and more independent and eventually you can feel it more and more clearly.

The more independent the spirit becomes, the more the relationship between magician and spirit becomes a form of splitting of consciousness: The spirit is a part of the magician, but at the same time it is also independent – and develops, the older it gets, a greater and greater independence. This can finally lead to the fact that the spirit begins to suck life force independently – which is not at all a desirable effect.

From a purely technical point of view, this spirit is a split-off part of the psyche and the life force body of the magician, which he has banished into the figure. The relationship between magician and spirit is the same as between magician and medium – a complete dominance and domination … at least this is what is strived for by the magician.

However, the hypnotist extends his consciousness to the hypnotized outside of himself, while the magician splits off a part of himself and forms it into an independent spirit. In extreme cases, the magician thereby destabilizes his own psyche.

This technique is also well known from fantasy literature: In the "Harry Potter" series, it appears in the form of horcruxes.

Such ghosts sometimes also arise unintentionally – especially during adolescent puberty. They then become poltergeists, which make some noise and can occasionally speak or move things, but which then also dissipate after a while.

However, a poltergeist is not quite as dramatic as one might think – in my parents' house we once had such a poltergeist for half a year and got used to it quite quickly. He then had a similar position as a pet. In the castle in the village where I live today, there were also several poltergeists for many years – they were quite old. Fortunately, together with a friend, I succeeded in calming down these ghosts and escorting them into the hereafter, so that it is now peaceful in the castle.

A Spiritus familiaris is, if one considers it purely technically, a willfully produced poltergeist.

If the Spiritus familiaris, which one has produced oneself, has become too strong or too independent, or if one wants to get rid of it for some other reason, one must dissolve it. To do this, you drain it of its life force, burn a note with its name and destroy the figure. This is not as easy as it sounds at first – this process feels like murdering a beloved pet or cutting away on's own arm …

Probably it would make more sense to re-integrate the Spiritus familiaris into one's own psyche – but I didn't think of this at that time and today I have no need to create such a spirit anymore, so I can't check how such a re-integration of a Spiritus familiaris into one's own psyche feels.

If such a spirit has become strong enough, it could also be that it defends itself telepathically and telekinetically against its destruction – I have experienced this with consecrated magic rings in a rather violent way. The repertoire of resistance of these "objects charged with life force" ranges from car crashes to trees falling down in calm weather without winds to objects returning to me several times after I had thrown them away.

This effect can also be read in "The Lord of the Rings", where it is described in connection with the attempt to destroy the "One Ring" and also in "Harry Potter", where the horcruxes fight against their destruction.

VIII 8.   A Levitation Experiment

There is a simple levitation experiment. For this one needs five persons. One of them sits down on a chair, the other four stand around him.

The four people hold their hands horizontally with the palms down next to each other, clench their fingers into two fists and then stretch only the two index fingers forward, touching each other along their entire length. Then the four standing people put their index fingers under the two armpits and under the two knees of the seated person and try to lift him up – which will most likely not succeed.

Next, the four standing people place their hands on top of the sitter's head (hand on hand on hand …) and sing a note together – simply an "a" at any pitch. Now the lifting of the sitter is repeated with the help of the index fingers – which now succeeds effortlessly, since the sitter no longer seems to have any weight.

In this experiment, by placing their hands on the sitter's head and by singing, the four standing people extend their own consciousness to the sitter and can then lift him up – just as they could move their own bodies.

VIII 9. The "Hepp" Experiment

The "Hepp attempt" works similarly to the levitation attempt. "Hepp" ist a German word and signifies "Come on!", "Jump!", and "Now!".

Person A lies down with her stomach on the ground and puts his arms next to her body or next to her head. Person B lies down with his belly across the calves of person A. Both persons together now look approximately like a "T".

Person A now tries to lift person B up with his legs – which usually will not be possible. Person A should take care of her legs and not get a muscle strain by doggedly overexerting herself.

Then person A imagines that from her head to her feet flows a ray of white light, which splits into two rays in her buttocks. Then Person A imagines that Person B is just a small pillow that is as light as a feather-cloud. Now person A inwardly says "Hepp!" while lifting person B with her calves – and person B will in all probability roll over person A's back with some momentum …

Again, person A has extended his consciousness to person B by "defining" that person B has only the weight of a small pillow. Apparently, the "definition" of the properties of person B by person A actually temporarily changes the properties of person B.

The expansion of consciousness used by the hypnotist to produce the hypnotic state in his counterpart apparently has very far-reaching effects – and is a central element in any form of magic.

VIII 10.   A Shaolin Experiment

The Shaolin monks have explored the possibilities of the body and consciousness very thoroughly in order to develop from them a weaponless art of self-defense. As a result, they can do many amazing things that would normally be considered impossible.

A simple example of this is the following experiment, which requires three people:

Person A places their hand, clenched into a fist, on a platform that reaches about to their waist – this can be a thick fence post, a wall, a rock, or something similar.

The other two people now hold on to person A's hand. Person A now tries with all his might to step forward from the pedestal, but he will not succeed because the other two people are holding his hand hard to the pedestal.

Now person A stops, relaxes, holds her free hand in front of her at eye level and looks into her palm – and simply walks off, pulling the people holding her hand behind her.

Here, as in the "Hepp" experiment, person A has defined the situation – or in other words, she has extended her consciousness to the other two persons.

Person A looks into her hand, i.e. she does not see anymore that the two other persons are holding her or simply does not pay attention to them anymore, but is completely with her decision to leave – and simply leaves, because she has defined the situation that way. Person A has thus extended his consciousness to the whole situation and can therefore define the situation and consequently act as he wants to.

From a purely technical point of view, what the Shaolin monk is doing is a wordless group hypnosis.

VIII 11.   Advertising and propaganda

You may also count the more cunning forms of advertising as a kind of hypnosis. Often it is not obvious at first glance how a special advertising works – there are often assoziations and suggestions hidden in the picture and in the text of the advertisment. They shall prompt the customer to buy the product.

The same goes for some political speeches, where the speaker attemps with much skill to dominate the listeners. In these cases often parades, buildings, gatherings, music, uniforms and so on are used to achieve the desired effct.

It's not hypnosis in the strict sense, but the effect can be very similar: people do things which they have not consciously dicided to do.

IX A Hypnosis Model

Hypnosis and remote hypnosis, as well as telepathy and telekinesis, and also much of the various magical phenomena, are most easily explained by assuming that consciousness is not limited to the body.

There are various forms of transference of consciousness: in healing, in consecrating objects, in Feng Shui, in initiations of people, in making house spirits, in battle magic, etc. These various forms of transference or expansion of consciousness show that when the consciousness has expanded to another object or body, it is able to move this object or body as if it were its own body, and in some cases even to define the characteristics of the "taken over body" such as its weight.

In the hypnosis model presented below, which is also a general magic model, there are four types of interaction:

- body acts on body	=> causal effect
- body acts on consciousness	=> perception, reaction
- consciousness acts on body	=> guidance, decision
- consciousness acts on consciousness	=> magic effect

These four interactions can be represented in a diagram as follows:

Interactions		
person 1		*person 2*
consciousness	↔	consciousness
↕		↕
body	↔	body

During hypnosis, the hypnotist extends his consciousness to the hypnotized person. In the graphic just shown, that looks like this:

Hypnosis		
Hypnotist		*Hypnotized*
consciousness	→ → →	consciousness
body		body

When the hypnotist gives a command to the hypnotized in normal hypnosis or telepathically in remote hypnosis or completely takes over the control of another's body as in combat magic, for example, the hypnotist extends his influence to the hypnotized's body as well – he temporarily takes over the other's body:

Hypnosis		
Hypnotist		*Hypnotized*
consciousness	→ → →	consciousness
		↓ ↓ ↓
body		body

The diagram for making a spiritus familiaris looks the same: The magician transfers part of his consciousness (and life force) to the form created from wax and clay.

- - -

Good luck and much prudence in your hypnosis experiments!

English Books by Harry Eilenstein

- Living Magic (261 p.)	- Mandalas for Beginners
- The Synthesis of Physics and Magic (192 p.)	- Money Magic for Beginners
- Astral Projection for Beginners (60 p.)	- Love Magic for Beginners
- Invocations for Beginners (52 p.)	- Magic Research for Beginners
- Evocations for Beginners (62 p.)	- Self-awareness for Beginners
- Auto-Movement for Beginners (60 p.)	- Symbolism of Numbers for Beginners
- Elves for Beginners (56 p.)	- Language of the Moon – for Beginners
- Hypnosis for Beginners (56 p.)	- Magic Chant for Beginners
These books will be puplished soon:	- Prophecy for Beginners
- Telepathy for Beginners	- Shamanism for Beginners
- Telepathy for Advanced Learners	- Magic Objects for Beginners
- Telekinesis for Beginners	- Da'ath-Magic for Beginners
- Life Force for Beginners	- Crop Circles for Beginners
- Meditation for Beginners	- Feng Shui for Beginners
- Kundalini for Beginners	- Magic for Beginners – Anthology I
- Chakra-Magic for Beginners	- Magic for Beginners – Anthology II
- Astrology for Beginners	- Magic for Beginners – Anthology III
- Ritual Magic for Beginners	- Magic for Beginners – Anthology IV

Bücher von Harry Eilenstein

Religion allgemein
- Die sieben Schritte des Lebens (428 S.)
- Muttergöttin und Schamanen (168 S.)
- Göbekli Tepe (472 S.)
- Die Göttin von Göbekli Tepe (144 S.)
- Totempfähle (440 S.)
- Christus (60 S.)
- Dakini (80 S.)
- Vajra (76 S.)

Ägypten
- Hathor und Re 1: Götter und Mythen im Alten Ägypten (432 S.)
- Hathor und Re 2: Die altägyptische Religion – Ursprünge, Kult und Magie (396 S.)
- Isis (508 S.)

Indogermanen
- Die Entwicklung der indogermanischen Religionen (700 S.)
- Wurzeln und Zweige der indogermanischen Religion (224 S.)

Germanen
- Die Götter der Germanen (87 Bände – siehe nächste Seite)
- Odin (300 S.)

Kelten
- Cernunnos (690 S.)
- Taliesin (228 S.)
- Der Kessel von Gundestrup (220 S.)
- Der Chiemsee-Kessel (76)

Psychologie
- Über die Freude (100 S.)
- Das Geheimnis des inneren Friedens (252 S.)
- Das Beziehungsmandala (52 S.)
- Gefühle und ihre Verwandlungen (404 S.)
- einsgerichtet (140 S.)
- Liebe und Eigenständigkeit (216 S.)
- Von innerer Fülle zu äußerem Gedeihen (52 S.)

Heilung
- Die Symbolik der Krankheiten (76 S.)

Kunst
- Herz des Tanzes – Tanz des Herzens (160 S.)

Drama
- König Athelstan (104 S.)

Bücher von Harry Eilenstein

„Magie für Anfänger"

- Telepathie für Anfänger (60 S.)
- Telepathie für Fortgeschrittene (52 S.)
- Telekinese für Anfänger (52 S.)
- Lebenskraft für Anfänger (60 S.)
- Meditation für Anfänger (56 S.)
- Kundalini für Anfänger (100 S.)
- Hypnose für Anfänger (56 S.)
- Auto-Movement für Anfänger (56 S.)
- Chakra-Magie für Anfänger (148 S.)
- Astralreisen für Anfänger (56 S.)
- Astrologie für Anfänger (120 S.)
- Ritual-Magie für Anfänger (56 S.)
- Mandalas für Anfänger (68 S.)
- Geldzauber für Anfänger (56 S.)
- Liebeszauber für Anfänger (52 S.)
- Invokationen für Anfänger (52 S.)
- Evokationen für Anfänger (60 S.)
- Elfen für Anfänger (56 S.)
- Magie-Forschung für Anfänger (140 S.)
- Selbsterkenntnis für Anfänger (52 S.)
- Zahlensymbolik für Anfänger (60 S.)
- Die Sprache des Mondes – für Anfänger (116 S.)
- Zaubergesänge für Anfänger (100 S.)
- Zukunftschau für Anfänger (60 S.)
- Schamanismus für Anfänger (52 S.)
- Magische Gegenstände für Anfänger (68 S.)
- Da'ath-Magie für Anfänger (64 S.)
- Kornkreise für Anfänger (348 S.)
- Feng Shui für Anfänger (96 S.)
- Magie für Anfänger – Sammelband I (696 S.)
- Magie für Anfänger – Sammelband II (664 S.)
- Magie für Anfänger – Sammelband III (580 S.)

„Traumreisen"

- Traumreisen zu Heilpflanzen (700 S.)

Magie

- Handbuch für Zauberlehrlinge (408 S.)
- Tarot (104 S.)
- Physik und Magie (184 S.)
- Die Synthese von Physik und Magie (200S.)
- Die Magie-Formel (156 S.)
- Krafttiere – Tiergöttinnen – Tiertänze (112 S.)
- Schwitzhütten (524 S.)
- Mythen und Magie der Harfe (116 S.)
- Magie heute – Berichte aus der Praxis (288 S.)

Meditation

- Der Lebenskraftkörper (230 S.)
- Die Chakren (100 S.)
- Das Chakren-System mit den Nebenchakren (296 S.)
- Organe und Chakren (64 S.)
- Die platonischen Körper in den Chakren (156 S.)
- Meditation (140 S.)
- Drachenfeuer (124 S.)
- Kundalini I (676 S.)
- Reinkarnation (156 S.)
- einsgerichtet (140 S.)

Astrologie

- Astrologie (496 S.)
- Photo-Astrologie (428 S.)
- Die astrologischen Aspekte (88 S.)
- Horoskop und Seele (120 S.)

Kabbala

- Kursus der praktischen Kabbala (150 S.)
- Eltern der Erde (450 S.)
- Blüten des Lebensbaumes:
    - Die Struktur des kabbalistischen Lebensbaumes (370 S.)
    - Der kabbalistische Lebensbaum als Forschungshilfsmittel (580 S.)
    - Der kabbalistische Lebensbaum als spirituelle Landkarte (520 S.)

Die Themen der 87 Bände der Reihe „Die Götter der Germanen"

1. Die Entwicklung der germanischen Religion	44. Die Symbolik der Wassertiere und sonstigen Tiere
2. Lexikon der germanischen Religion	
3. Der ursprüngliche Göttervater Tyr	45. Die Symbolik der Pflanzen
4. Tyr in der Unterwelt: der Schmied Wieland	46. Die Symbolik der Farben
5. Tyr in der Unterwelt: der Riesenkönig Teil 1	47. Die Symbolik der Zahlen
6. Tyr in der Unterwelt: der Riesenkönig Teil 2	48. Die Symbolik von Sonne, Mond und Sternen
7. Tyr in der Unterwelt: der Zwergenkönig	49.a Das Jenseits I – Das Hügelgrab
8. Der Himmelswächter Heimdall	49.b Das Jenseits II – Der Jenseitsweg
9. Der Sommergott Baldur	50. Seelenvogel, Utiseta und Einweihung
10. Der Meeresgott: Ägir, Hler und Njörd	51. Wiederzeugung und Wiedergeburt
11. Der Eibengott Ullr	52. Elemente der Kosmologie
12. Die Zwillingsgötter Alcis	53. Der Weltenbaum
13. Der neue Göttervater Odin Teil 1	54. Die Symbolik der Himmelsrichtungen und der Jahreszeiten
14. Der neue Göttervater Odin Teil 2	
15. Der Fruchtbarkeitsgott Freyr	55.a Mythologische Motive I
16. Der Chaos-Gott Loki	55.b Mythologische Motive II
17. Der Donnergott Thor	56. Der Tempel
18. Der Priestergott Hönir	57. Die Einrichtung des Tempels
19. Die Göttersöhne	58. Priesterin – Seherin – Zauberin – Hexe
20. Die unbekannteren Götter	59. Priester – Seher – Zauberer
21. Die Göttermutter Frigg	60. Rituelle Kleidung und Schmuck
22. Die Liebesgöttin: Freya und Menglöd	61. Skalden und Skaldinnen
23. Die Erdgöttinnen	62 Kriegerinnen und Ekstase-Krieger
24. Die Korngöttin Sif	63. Die Symbolik der Körperteile
25. Die Apfel-Göttin Idun	64.a Magie und Ritual I
26. Die Hügelgrab-Jenseitsgöttin Hel	64.b Magie und Ritual II
27. Die Meeres-Jenseitsgöttin Ran	64.c Magie und Ritual III
28. Die unbekannteren Jenseitsgöttinnen	65. Gestaltwandlungen
29. Die unbekannteren Göttinnen	66.a Magische Angriffs-Waffen
30. Die Nornen	66.b Magische Verteidigungs-Waffen
31. Die Walküren	67. Magische Werkzeuge und Gegenstände
32. Die Zwerge	68. Zaubersprüche
33. Der Urriese Ymir	69. Göttermet
34. Die Riesen	70. Zaubertränke
35. Die Riesinnen	71. Träume, Omen und Orakel
36. Mythologische Wesen	72. Runen
37. Mythologische Priester und Priesterinnen	73. Sozial-religiöse Rituale
38. Sigurd/Siegfried	74. Weisheiten und Sprichworte
39. Helden und Göttersöhne	75. Kenningar
40. Die Symbolik der Vögel und Insekten	76. Rätsel
41. Die Symbolik der Schlangen, Drachen und Ungeheuer	77. Die vollständige Edda des Snorri Sturluson
	78. Frühe Skaldenlieder
42.a Die Symbolik der Herdentiere I	79.a Mythologische Sagas I
42.b Die Symbolik der Herdentiere II	79.b Mythologische Sagas II
43. Die Symbolik der Raubtiere	80. Hymnen an die germanischen Götter